BULLETIN BOARDS
for Sunday School

Publisher	*Arthur L. Miley*
Author	*Carolyn Passig Jensen*
Art Director	*Debbie Birch*
Cover Design	*Gary Zupkas*
Production Director	*Barbara Bucher*
Production Assistant	*Valerie Fetrow*
Illustrator	*Fran Kizer*
Production Artist	*Nelson Beltran*
Proofreader	*Barbara Bucher*

Rainbow Publishers
Copyright © 1997 • Eighth Printing
Rainbow Books • P.O. Box 261129 • San Diego, CA 92196

#RB36192
ISBN 0-937282-34-0

CONTENTS

Introduction

Children learn best and remember more when they can see and visualize what they are taught. In fact, we learn 83 percent by sight and only 12 percent by hearing and touch together. But when hearing, touch *and* sight are combined, learning is much easier and effective.

Bulletin boards are a very effective way to teach children important biblical concepts so they will remember them. Because bulletin boards are colorful and attention-getting, children are naturally drawn to them and to the lessons they teach.

Today, bulletin boards are far more than simply boards to hold announcements and notices. Think of bulletin boards as an important part of your Sunday school or Bible classroom for several reasons:

- Bulletin boards are simple, inexpensive and colorful ways to decorate your classroom and provide an attractive learning environment
- Bulletin boards help children visualize and remember important spiritual concepts far longer than just talking about them
- Bulletin boards stimulate discussion and learning of Bible truths
- Bulletin boards help focus children's attention on important concepts you want to teach
- Bulletin boards help relate spiritual concepts to the children's everyday lives
- Bulletin boards motivate children to think critically and creatively
- Bulletin boards display useful information, announcements and invitations
- Bulletin boards provide an opportunity for children and teachers to relate to each other as they construct bulletin boards together

This book (and the other three books in this series) contain 13 seasonal Bible bulletin boards which can help you effectively teach biblical concepts in the ways listed above. The patterns and instructions in this book make it easy to construct these delightful bulletin boards, and you won't need a lot of artistic talent to be successful either!

That's because each bulletin board includes complete instructions and suggestions for borders, background, materials and how to put everything together. Full-size patterns are also provided, as are large headline letters and three seasonal borders and corners. All patterns, letters and borders may be used right out of the book or traced, enlarged, reduced, duplicated or photocopied to make attractive classroom bulletin boards.

Each bulletin board also includes a suggested Bible Memory Verse for the class to learn together and ideas for using the bulletin board to teach important spiritual concepts. (The King James Version of the Bible is used unless noted otherwise.)

Each bulletin board is designed for use in Sunday schools. Many may also be used in kids clubs, Vacation Bible School, children's church, Christian schools or anywhere the Bible is taught. The age of children for which the bulletin board is appropriate is also noted.

So . . . turn your classroom into an exciting learning environment with the colorful seasonal Bible-teaching bulletin boards in this book!

How to Create Beautiful Bulletin Boards Using the Materials in this Book

Each of the 13 Bible-teaching bulletin boards for Winter in this book contains complete instructions and full-size patterns, lettering and seasonal borders and corners, plus instructions and suggestions for backgrounds and for putting the bulletin boards together. These four pages contain hints, tips and how-to's for using the materials in this book (and the other three books in this series) to create beautiful bulletin boards!

Backgrounds

Backgrounds are vital to the overall design of the bulletin board. In this book, simple suggestions are given for backgrounds for each bulletin board. Feel free to also experiment with materials you have on hand or which are readily available, such as:
- Textured fabrics: flannel, felt, burlap, cottons, cheesecloth
- Construction paper
- Crepe paper
- Wrapping paper, either solid color or with small print or design
- Colored tissue papers
- Newspapers
- Aluminum foil or foil-covered wrapping paper
- Brown paper bags crumpled and then flattened
- Bamboo or grass place mats or floor mats
- Colorful corrugated paper available from school supply stores
- Butcher paper
- Poster board on which figures can be permanently attached
- Maps
- Adhesive-backed plastic in a variety of colors or patterns

You may wish to choose one background which you can use for several bulletin boards during the season.

Borders

Borders make the bulletin board, so after your background is in place, it's time to frame your bulletin board with an attractive, colorful border. Three seasonal borders and matching corners are provided on pages 62 and 63 of this book for use with selected bulletin boards in this book. Other simple border suggestions are given with the remaining bulletin boards in this book.

To use the seasonal borders and corners on pages 62 and 63, duplicate enough copies of the border strip to frame the entire bulletin board. Also make four copies of the matching corner. (Corners can also be used by themselves, or with strips of construction paper forming the border.)

You may duplicate the border and corner on white paper and have the children color the border with markers. (Markers give brighter colors than crayons, so are preferable for all bulletin board work), or you may wish to reproduce the border and corner onto colored paper. (See "Duplicating Patterns and Lettering" below.)

Overlap the border strips slightly and glue or tape the sections together. Use double faced tape to attach the border and corners directly to the frame of the bulletin board or staple the border and corners to the edge of the bulletin board just inside the frame. Roll the border to store for future use.

Attractive borders can also be made with the following materials attached to the frame of the bulletin board:

- Artificial flowers, real or artificial leaves, nature items
- Rope or twine
- Braided yarn
- Wide gift-wrap ribbon
- Purchased corrugated borders available from school supply stores
- Strips of twisted crepe paper 3/4 inch wide
- Strips of construction paper cut in attractive shapes, such as scallops, zig-zags, fringes, etc.

Making Bulletin Boards Three-Dimensional

Although bulletin boards are normally flat, there are many imaginative ways you can add a three-dimensional effect to your bulletin boards. Many of the bulletin boards in this book already include ideas for three-dimensional effects, but here are more you may like to try:

- Put a cork, thick piece of cardboard, or styrofoam behind figures or lettering
- Attach large figures to the bulletin board by curving them slightly outward from the board
- Glue or attach three-dimensional or textured objects such as cotton balls, small pieces of wood, twigs, nature items, feathers, yarn, children's toys, small clothing objects (like scarves and mittens), balloons, artificial flowers or leaves, chenille wire, fabrics and burlap, bamboo or woven place mats, corrugated paper, sandpaper, crumpled aluminum foil or grocery bags, rope, drinking straws, and such
- Use artificial spray snow for a winter scene
- "Stuff" figures by putting crumpled newspaper or paper towels behind the figures before attaching to the bulletin board
- Flowers can be made from individual sections cut from egg cartons
- Heavy objects (such as a small tree branch or a toy) may be mounted securely in the following way: Cut two or more strips of bias binding tape or ribbon (available from fabric stories). Securely staple one end of the bias tape to the bulletin board, place around the item to be mounted and staple the other end (above the object) to the bulletin board so the object hangs securely on the bias tape straps.

Lettering

Each bulletin board in this book includes full-sized lettering which is to be used with the full-size patterns to create your bulletin board. To use the lettering, you may do the following:

- Cut the lettering out of any paper. Place the page(s) of lettering from this book over the sheet(s) of paper out of which you want to cut the letters. Cut through both sheets, using scissors or a craft knife. Mount letters individually on the bulletin board.
- Duplicate the lettering onto white paper and color in the letters with markers.
- Duplicate the lettering onto white or colored construction paper or copy machine paper. Cut the words apart and mount each word on the bulletin board in strip form.
- Trace the lettering onto paper of any color using colored markers. Cut out individual letters or cut apart words and use in strip form.
- Cut individual letters out of two colors of paper at once. When mounting letters on the bulletin board, lay one color on top of the other and offset the bottom letter slightly so it creates a shadow effect.

Attractive lettering can also be made by cutting letters out of wallpaper, fabrics, felt, adhesive-backed plastic in various colors or patterns, wrapping paper, grocery bags which have been crumpled and then flattened, old newspapers and other materials. For a professional look, outline letters with a dark marker for a neat edge and good contrast. Always try to use dark colors for lettering.

Textures can be used for lettering also, either by cutting the letters out of textured materials or by gluing on glitter, sequins, straw, twigs, yarn, rope, lace, craft or ice cream sticks, chenille wire or other materials.

To mount letters flat, staple to the board, use double-sided tape or roll a small piece of tape to make it double-sided. Always put the tape under the letter so it does not show.

Position letters either in a straight line or in a curved or staggered arrangement. Space letters attractively.

Duplicating Patterns and Lettering

All patterns, lettering, borders and corners in this book may be used right out of the book or traced, enlarged, reduced, duplicated or photocopied to make attractive classroom bulletin boards.

The easiest way to duplicate the materials in this book is to use a copy machine to simply copy the patterns, lettering or borders onto white or colored copy machine paper. (Copy machine paper is available in a wide variety of colors ranging from pastel colors to very bright colors.) For a very nominal price you can copy onto these colored papers at most copy centers. Construction paper also works in some copy machines.

You can also trace materials in this book onto white or colored paper by holding the page you wish to trace up to a window or by using carbon paper.

You can also color the materials from this book with markers.

The easiest way to reduce or enlarge materials is to use a copy machine which enlarges or reduces, available at most copy centers also.

You can also trace the items you wish to enlarge onto a overhead projector transparency, project the transparency onto a sheet of paper on a wall, adjusting the image to the size you wish, and trace the image onto the white or colored paper. An opaque projector can also be used to enlarge patterns without having to trace them onto transparency material.

Mounting Materials on Your Bulletin Board

It is important that all materials stay securely on your bulletin board until you wish to take them down. Stapling materials directly to the bulletin board is the most secure method of mounting most materials and the staples are virtually unnoticeable. Be sure to have a staple puller handy to help prevent frustration and broken fingernails. Staples are also much better for bulletin boards for small children as it is quite difficult to pull a staple out of the bulletin board, unlike pins and tacks. Be sure no loose staples are left on the floor after you finish putting up the bulletin board.

Pins can be used if you wish to support the materials rather than make holes. Double-faced tape, or tape rolled to make it double faced is also effective. For heavier materials, use carpet tape or packing tape.

How to Make Your Bulletin Boards Durable and Reusable

Cover both sides of your bulletin board figures with clear adhesive-backed plastic. Cut around the figures, leaving a 1/4 inch edge of plastic. (If one figure is made up of several parts, put the parts together before covering with the plastic.) You can also glue figures to colored construction paper and cut around the figure, leaving a narrow border of construction paper.

Teaching with the Bulletin Boards

Each of the bulletin boards in this book includes a suggested Bible Memory Verse and teaching tips to help you use the bulletin boards to teach important biblical concepts to your students.

In addition, children 8 years and older enjoy helping with the construction of the bulletin boards and are delighted to help cut, color, glue and staple. This provides a great opportunity for the message of the board to "soak in" while the children and teacher get to know each other better as they work together. The more the children are involved in constructing the bulletin boards, the better and more effective their learning will be.

Appropriate for ages 4 to 12

Background and Border:

Cover bulletin board with blue paper, fabric or felt. Use white scalloped border.

Materials and Instructions:

Trace and cut the figures of Mary, Joseph, Baby Jesus, manger, donkey and lamb from pages 12 and 13 out of paper or felt, using the following colors: Mary — light blue or yellow; Joseph — burgundy; Baby Jesus — white; manger — brown or gold; donkey — brown or light grey; lamb — white, light grey or black. (Felt is preferable to paper for the figures and lettering.) Cut a star reduced from the star pattern on page 37 out of gold or yellow felt. Cover with glitter.

Attach all figures in place on bulletin board according to illustration above.

Duplicate letters from page 11 onto white paper or cut out of felt. Position on bulletin board.

(These figures and lettering are also very attractive made into a felt banner for display in your church sanctuary or other area. Figures and lettering can be easily enlarged if desired.)

Teaching with this Bulletin Board:

Use this bulletin board to help teach the Christmas story. Talk about the humble stable in which Jesus was born and the animals likely nearby. Then discuss why Christ's birth is an event in which we rejoice. Learn the Bible Memory Verse together. Older children may wish to learn the entire passage of Luke 2:1-20.

Suggested Bible Memory Verse:

"For unto you is born this day in the city of David a Saviour, which is Christ the Lord." — Luke 2:11

10

Rejoice!

Christ

is Born!

Baby Jesus: Trace and cut out of white paper or felt

Lamb: Trace and cut out of white, light grey or black paper or felt.

Donkey: Trace and cut out of brown or dark grey paper or felt.

12

Manger:
Trace and cut out of brown or gold paper or felt

Mary:
Trace and cut out of light blue or yellow paper or felt

Joseph:
Trace and cut out of burgundy paper or felt

13

Appropriate for ages 4 to 12

Background and Border:

Cover bulletin board with dark green paper or fabric. Dark green Christmas wrapping paper with a small design works nicely too. Duplicate the Christmas border and corner from pages 62 and 63 onto colored paper and cover portions with glitter. Or duplicate the border and corner onto white paper and color with markers.

Materials and Instructions:

Use 9 inch white paper plates as faces for carolers. Cut mouths, traced from page 17, out of red or pink construction paper or felt and glue to paper plates. Duplicate two eyes for each caroler from page 17 onto white paper, color with markers and glue in place. If desired, lightly rub powdered blush on the plates to represent pink cheeks. Glue on yarn for hair.

Duplicate collar from page 16 onto white paper and cut out. Glue under rim of paper plate. Trace the bow tie from page 17 onto red construction paper or felt and cut out. Glue on top of white collar.

Staple carolers to the bulletin board.

Cut several musical notes out of black construction paper or felt and mount on board near carolers. (Ovals cut out of black construction paper could be glued to black chenille wire to form notes also.)

Cut lettering from page 15 out of gold foil-covered wrapping paper or gold construction paper or felt. Mount in place. If desired, duplicate the lettering onto gold paper and use in strip form.

Teaching with this Bulletin Board:

Talk about why Christmas and Jesus' birth is an event we celebrate. Ask the children to think of things which would be different if Jesus had not come to earth. Then help the children to thank God for Jesus' birth by saying short sentence prayers of thanksgiving. Learn the Bible Memory Verse together.

Suggested Bible Memory Verse:

"May all who seek You rejoice and be glad in You."
— Psalm 40:16 NIV

Rejoice!

It's

Christmas!

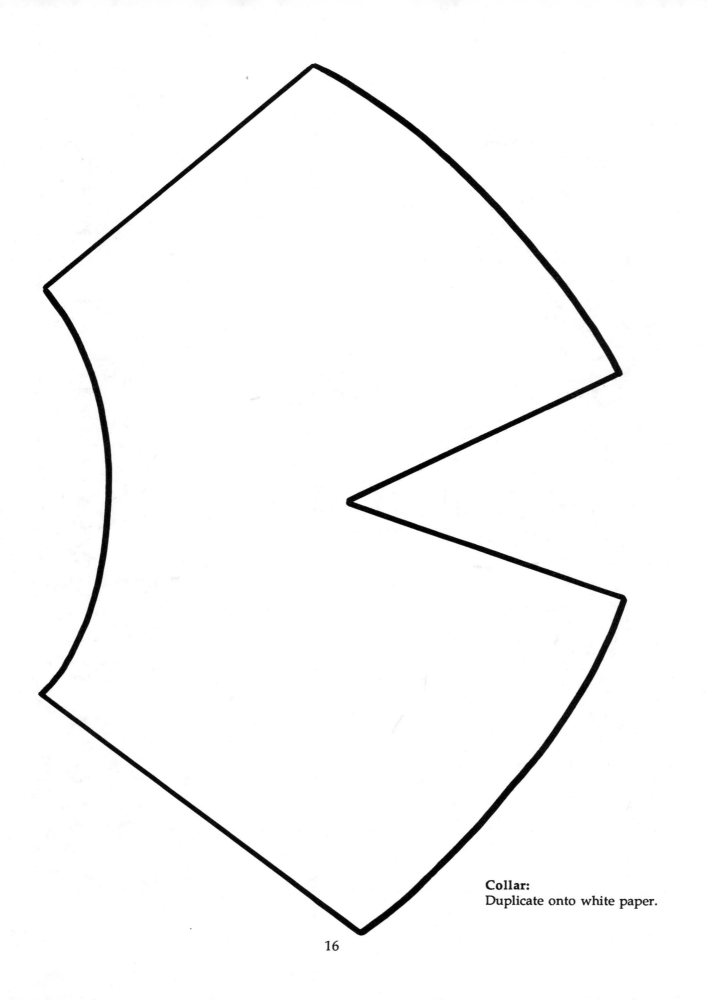

Collar:
Duplicate onto white paper.

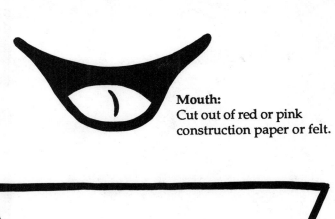

Mouth:
Cut out of red or pink
construction paper or felt.

Eyes:
Duplicate onto white paper,
cut out and color in pupils.

Bow tie:
Cut out of red paper or felt.

Musical note:
Cut out of black paper or felt.

Appropriate for ages 9 to 12

Background and Border:
Cover bulletin board with purple fabric or corrugated paper. Use gold scalloped border or twist two strips of crepe paper together to form border.

Materials and Instructions:
Use actual calendar pages for the bodies. Form arms and legs out of chenille wire and glue behind the calendar pages. Bend the ends of the wires into a circular shape to form hands and feet.

Staple the calendar pages to the bulletin board in sequence, leaving the calendar pages flat or roll them for a three-dimensional effect as shown above.

Duplicate 12 heads from page 19 onto white or colored paper. Color, if desired, and glue on yarn scraps for hair. Put actual ribbon bow in girls' hair. Staple one head above each calendar sheet.

Cut lettering from pages 20-21 out of yellow construction paper or duplicate onto yellow paper and use in strip form.

Teaching with this Bulletin Board:
Talk about ways we can live for Jesus all year. If time allows, you might talk about each month individually. Let the children think of a specific way they can live for Jesus in that month and write it on the calendar page for that month. Examples include: May — visit a elderly woman in a retirement home on Mother's Day; September — be friendly to a new child on the first day of school; December — give food for a Christmas basket for poor people. Learn the Bible Memory Verse together.

Suggested Bible Memory Verse:
"Do not forget to do good and to share" — Hebrews 13:16 NIV

Heads for calendar pages:
Duplicate 12 onto white or colored paper.
Color, if desired, and glue on yarn scraps for hair.

Happy

New Year!

Let's Live

for

Jesus

all Year!

21

Keys for a Happy New Year

Appropriate for ages 9 to 12

Background and Border:

Cover bulletin board with tan or light blue fabric or paper. Reduce keys from pages 24 and 25 and cut out of various colors of construction paper to border the bulletin board.

Materials and Instructions:

Cut keys on pages 24 and 25 out of various colors of construction paper. Cut one additional key out of gold foil-covered wrapping paper. Cut a large black ring out of construction paper or use several strands of chenille wire twisted together.

On each key, write one activity as shown above, or choose your own. On the gold key write "Accept Jesus as Savior." Staple keys and black ring into place on the bulletin board.

Cut lettering from page 23 out of gold or silver wrapping paper or construction paper to match the keys. Or duplicate the lettering onto colored paper and use in strip form. Position on bulletin board.

Teaching with this Bulletin Board:

Talk to the children about good things we should do which please Jesus. If desired, each child could write one thing on a key and then put their key on the bulletin board. Talk about each activity in turn, stressing to the children that these are good activities which please Jesus, but that the only way of salvation is to accept Jesus as Savior. (Point out that only this key is gold.) Explain the plan of salvation and give the children the opportunity to accept Jesus as Savior. Discuss and learn the Bible Memory Verse together.

Suggested Bible Memory Verse:

"For by grace are ye saved through faith; and that not of yourselves; it is the gift of God: Not of works." — Ephesians 2:8-9

Keys for a Happy New Year

Keys:
Cut several out of various colors of construction paper. Cut one key out of gold paper.

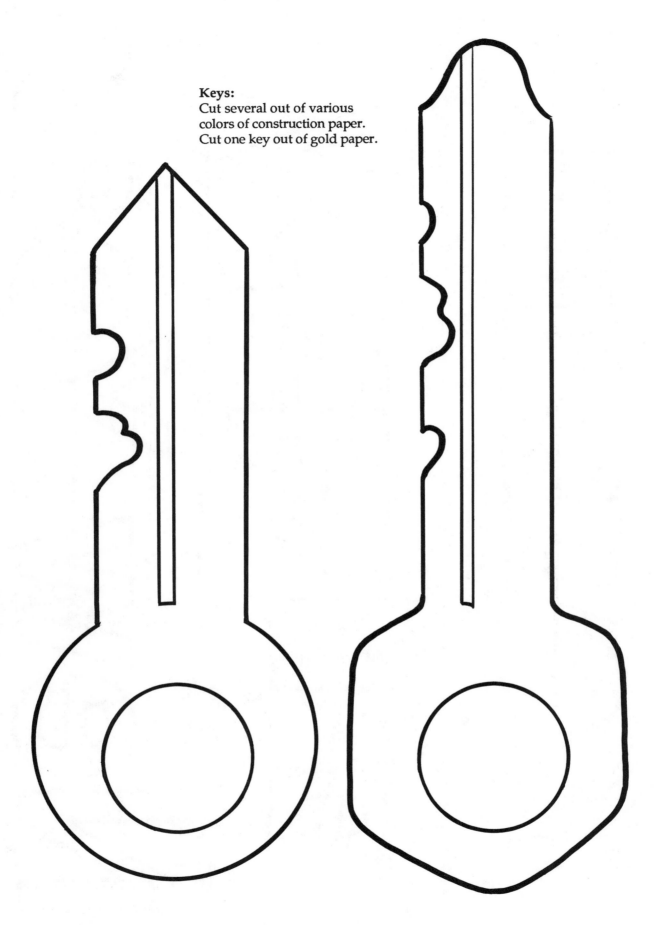

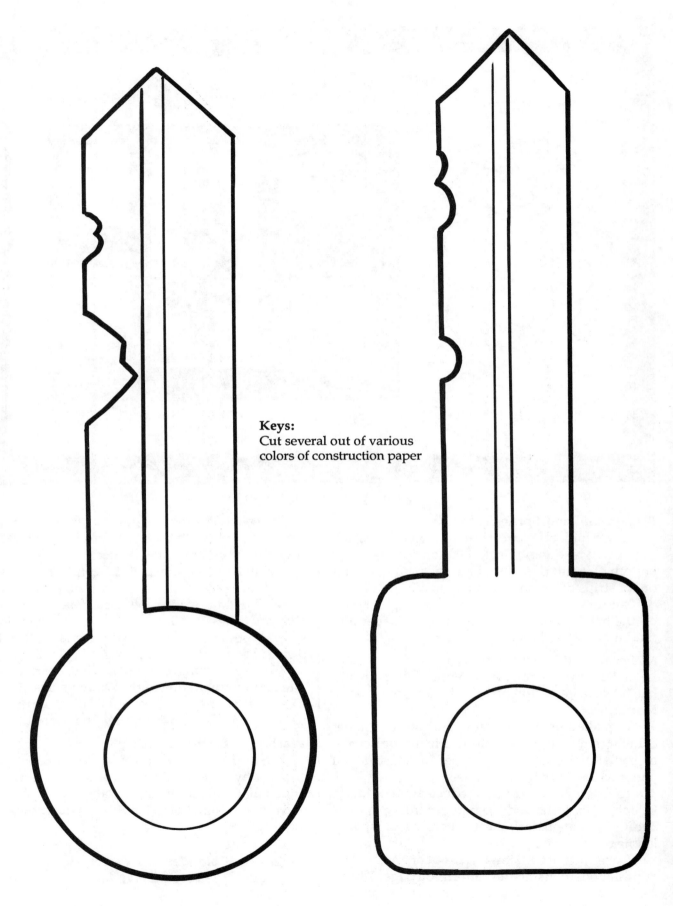

Keys:
Cut several out of various
colors of construction paper

25

Appropriate for ages 6 to 11

Background and Border:

Cover bulletin board with light blue fabric, felt or paper. Make snow drift of cotton batting along bottom of board. Use dark blue corrugated border or cut strips of construction paper.

Mount a large piece of dark blue poster board on the board. Cut five sheets of white paper and mount on poster board.

Materials and Instructions:

Follow instructions for making snowman and hat from page 54 to correct size for your board. Mount.

To make snowflakes, cut white plastic or paper drinking straws into three pieces. Pin through center of snowflake onto a dark sheet of construction paper in one of the white panels.

To make nativity scene, reduce and cut Mary, Joseph, Baby Jesus and the manger from pages 12 and 13. Mount on dark sheet of construction paper in one of the white panels.

Trace and cut Christmas tree out of green paper or poster board, using the patterns on pages 28 and 29. Decorate with glitter and sequins. Glue on star.

Cut trees along broken lines and fold along fold line. Fit together. Staple tree to board along folded edge for three-dimensional effect.

To make angel from page 27, duplicate face and cut out robe and wings according to instructions on page 27. Fold angel's robe back along fold lines, glue on wings and face and tape or glue folded sides of robe into rounded shape in one of the white panels. Form halo of silver or gold chenille wire.

Cut out several red, pink or white hearts, decorate and mount in one of the white panels.

Cut lettering from page 30 out of dark blue paper or felt. Cover with glitter and mount.

Teaching with this Bulletin Board:

Learn the Bible Memory Verse together. Talk about why God made winter and some of the things that happen during winter . Let each child name one thing about winter for which they are thankful.

Suggested Bible Memory Verse:

"Lord, . . .You created all things." — Revelation 4:11 NIV

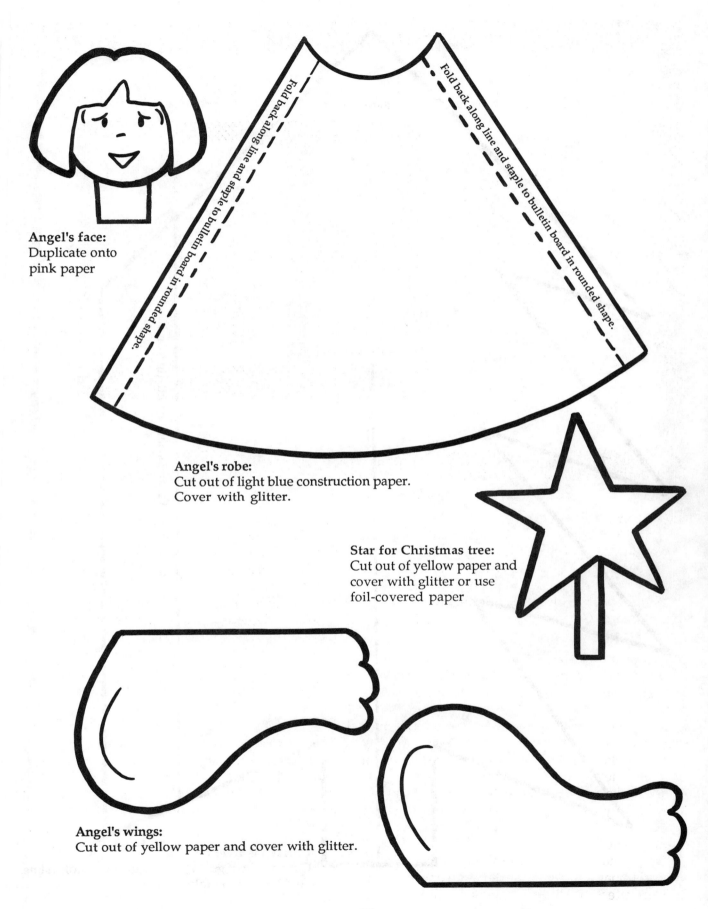

Angel's face:
Duplicate onto
pink paper

Angel's robe:
Cut out of light blue construction paper.
Cover with glitter.

Fold back along line and staple to bulletin board in rounded shape.

Fold back along line and staple to bulletin board in rounded shape.

Star for Christmas tree:
Cut out of yellow paper and
cover with glitter or use
foil-covered paper

Angel's wings:
Cut out of yellow paper and cover with glitter.

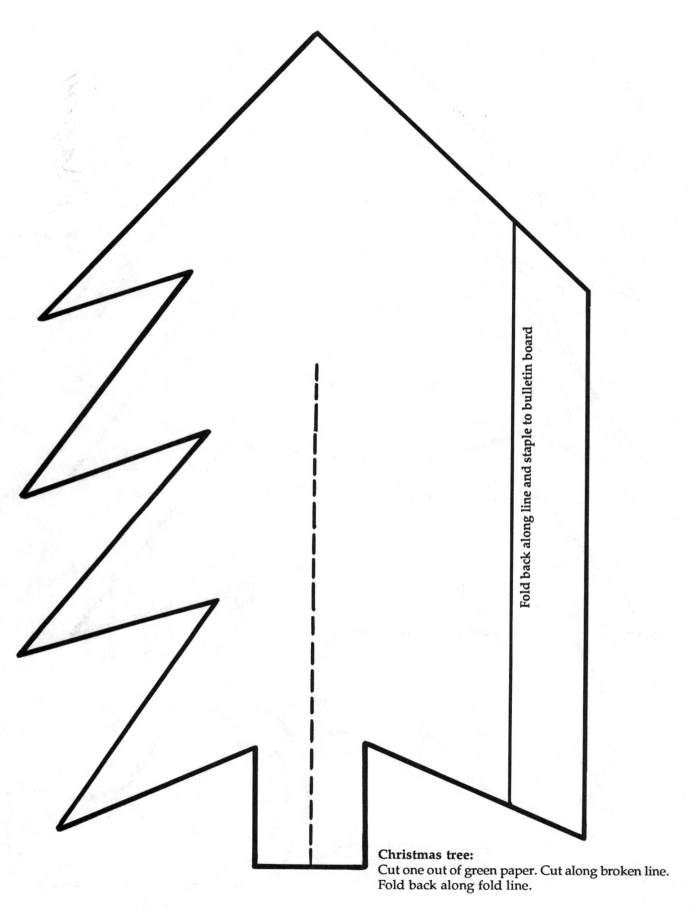

Fold back along line and staple to bulletin board

Christmas tree:
Cut one out of green paper. Cut along broken line.
Fold back along fold line.

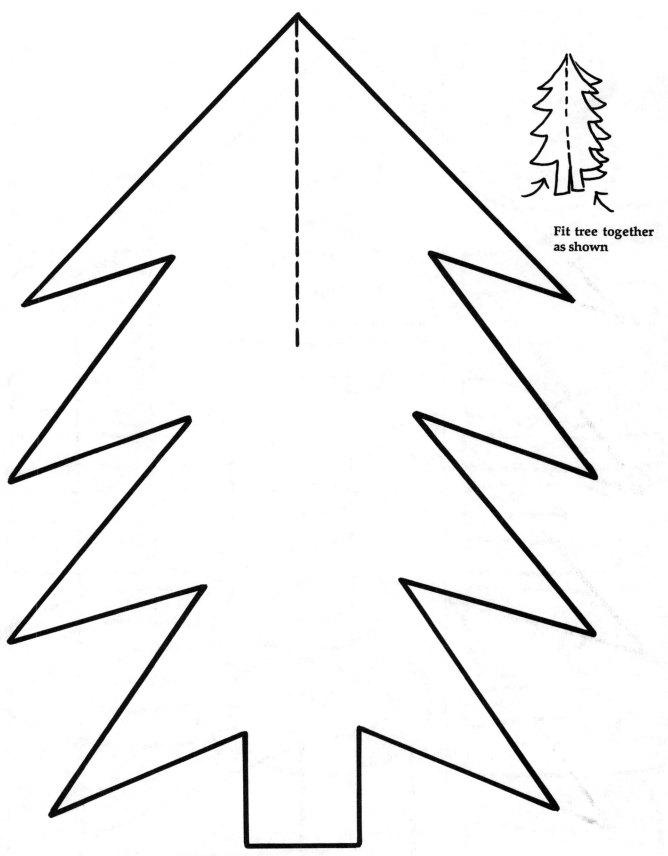

Fit tree together as shown

Christmas tree:
Cut one out of green paper. Cut along broken line.

Thank You

for

God for

Winter

Appropriate for ages 8 to 11

Background and Border:

Cover bulletin board with light blue paper or fabric. (Flannel fabric works nicely.) Make snow drift along the bottom of the board by stapling cotton batting to the board. (Stuff batting slightly with crumbled newspapers to give a three-dimensional effect.) Cut strips of cotton batting for the border or duplicate the Wintertime border and corner from pages 62 and 63 onto blue paper or onto white paper and color with markers.

Materials and Instructions:

Duplicate three penguins from pages 32 and 33 onto white paper. Glue on (or color in) orange beaks and attach moveable eyes. Duplicate penguin's feet onto gold paper and glue to the bottom of each penguin. Cut caps out of various colors of bright construction paper or fabric, or use the toes of old socks as caps.

Staple the penguins to the bulletin board.

Cut scarves for each penguin out of colorful fabric and staple to board also.

As shown above, for two of the penguins insert Bibles, which you have duplicated onto white paper and colored, into the slit cut along broken line in the penguin's wing.

Duplicate lettering from pages 34 and 35 onto dark blue felt or construction paper. Or duplicate lettering onto colored paper and use in strip form. Place in position on bulletin board.

Teaching with this Bulletin Board:

Talk about why it is important for Christians to attend Sunday school. Talk about some of the things we learn in Sunday school. Encourage the children to invite their friends. Emphasize that anyone is welcome in God's house. Learn the Bible Memory Verse together.

Suggested Bible Memory Verse:

"Let us go into the house of the Lord." — Psalm 122:1

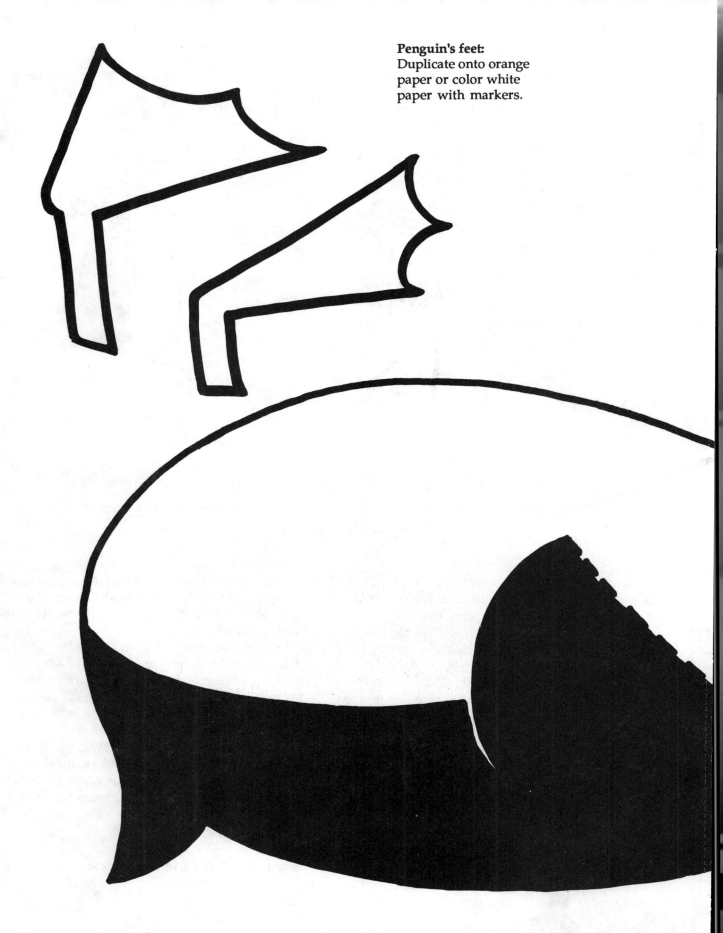

Penguin's feet:
Duplicate onto orange
paper or color white
paper with markers.

Penguin's Bible:
Duplicate two onto white
paper and color with markers.

Penguin's cap:
Cut out of brightly-colored
paper or fabric.

Penguin:
Duplicate three onto white paper.

Sunday School is for

Everyone!

Don't Miss

Out!

Our Love Gifts at Christmas

Appropriate for ages 7 to 12

Background and Border:

Cover bulletin board with white fabric or wrapping paper. Duplicate Christmas border and corner from pages 62 and 63 onto red paper or color with markers. (Light-colored Christmas wrapping paper with a small colorful print would also work well for the background.)

Materials and Instructions:

Cut large triangular-shaped Christmas tree out of green poster board. Staple to the board. Trace star from pattern on page 37 onto poster board and cover with foil or foil-covered wrapping paper. Cover with glitter. Mount on the board. See below for the gifts for the tree.

Trace and cut lettering from page 38 onto foil-covered wrapping paper and outline with a black marker. Or duplicate the lettering onto red paper and use in strip form.

Teaching with this Bulletin Board:

A few weeks before Christmas, give each child a sheet of construction paper. Instruct them to fold the construction paper to form a card. Inside the card they are to write a note to a specific person telling them something the child will do as a special gift. (This should be something the child can do for the person, not a gift he or she will buy.) You might suggest such things as mowing the lawn for a grandparent, walking the dog for a neighbor, vacuuming the living room for Mother, or helping clean the garage with Dad.) Discuss with the children the fact that some gifts are more precious than money or possessions.

The children may decorate their cards with drawings, or they may glue on Christmas ribbons, bows, and wrapping paper, or lace, glitter, yarn or other materials you provide to make the cards look like Christmas gifts. Let each child pin his or her card to the Christmas tree. After the last class before Christmas, allow each child to take his gift card home to give.

Discuss and learn the Bible Memory Verse.

Suggested Bible Memory Verse:

"God loveth a cheerful giver." —II Corinthians 9:7

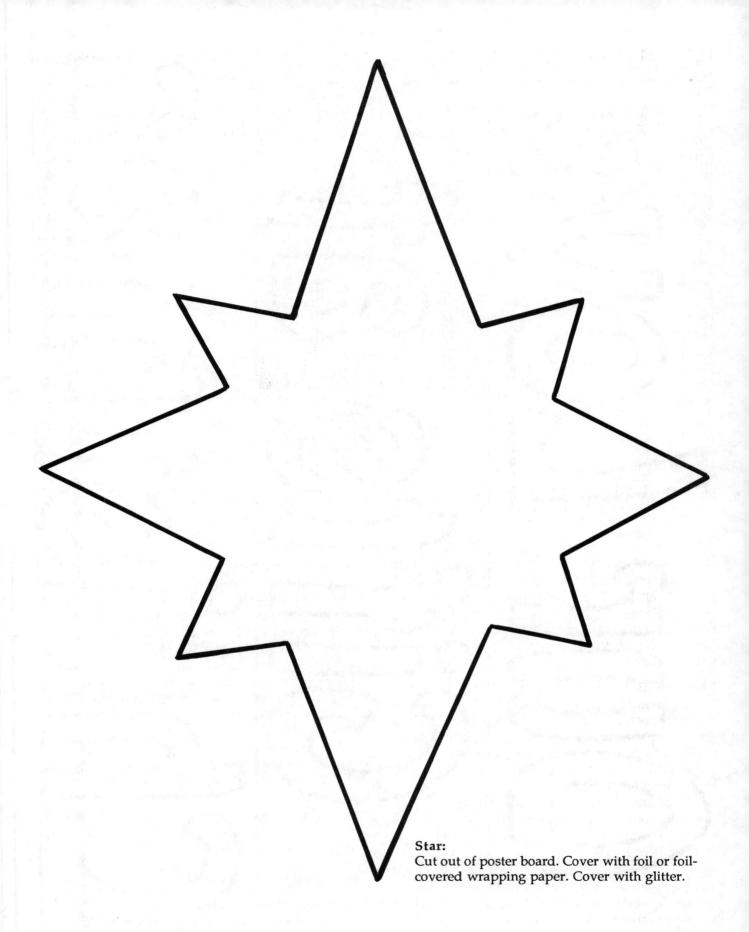

Star:
Cut out of poster board. Cover with foil or foil-covered wrapping paper. Cover with glitter.

Our Love

Gifts at

Christmas

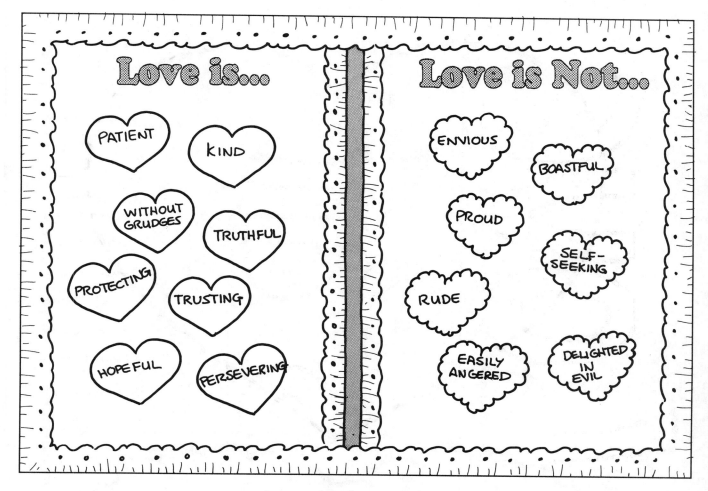

Appropriate for ages 10 to 12

Background and Border:

Cover bulletin board with white fabric or paper. (A fabric or wrapping paper with a tiny pink or red print on a white background would be very nice also.) Tape or staple white or pink ruffled lace trim around the edge of the bulletin board as border.

Down the middle of the board, staple two rows of ruffled lace trim. Cover inside edges with a piece of red, pink or white ribbon.

Materials and Instructions:

Duplicate 15 hearts from page 40 onto pink and red paper. On eight of the hearts write the attributes of love from 1 Corinthians 13 (NIV) (write one word or phrase on each heart): patient, kind, without grudges (keeps no record of wrongs), truthful (rejoices with the truth), protecting, trusting, hopeful, persevering.

On the other seven hearts write the word or phrases telling what love is not: envious, boastful, proud, rude, self-seeking, easily angered, delighted in evil.

Cut lettering from page 41 out of red construction paper or duplicate onto pink paper and use in strip form.

Teaching with this Bulletin Board:

Hold up each heart in turn. If the children do not know the meaning of each word, explain it and ask them to identify if it is or is not an attribute of love. Place the heart on the correct side of the bulletin board. Guide the children in learning the Scripture passage by pointing to each heart as the word is said.

Suggested Bible Memory Verses:

"Love is patient, love is kind. It does not envy, it does not boast, it is not proud. It is not rude, it is not self-seeking, it is not easily angered, it keeps no record of wrongs. Love does not delight in evil but rejoices with the truth. It always protects, always trusts, always hopes, always perseveres." — 1 Corinthians 13:4-7 NIV.

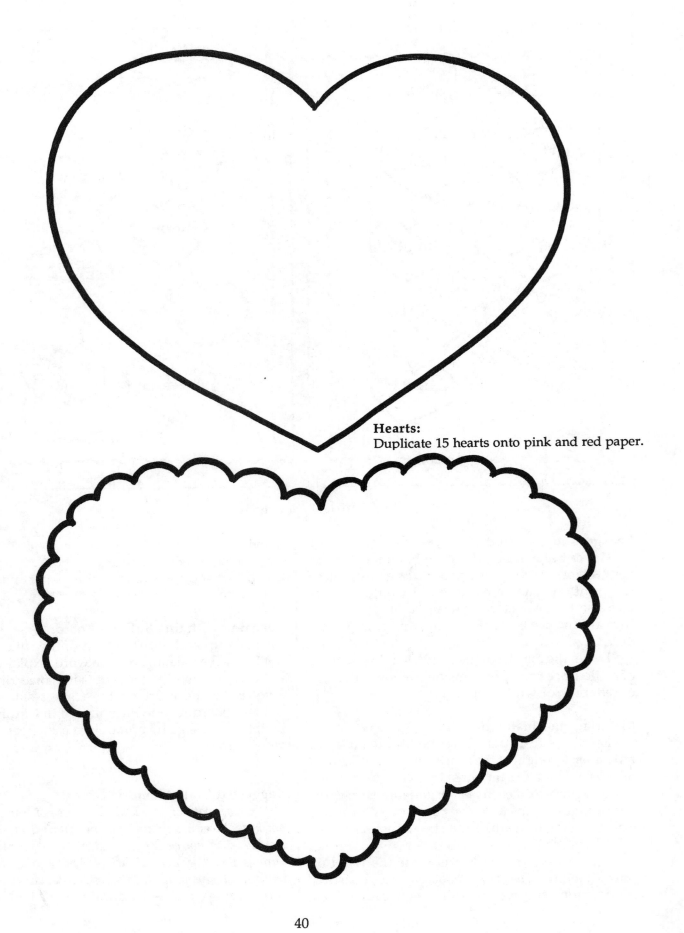

Hearts:
Duplicate 15 hearts onto pink and red paper.

Love is...

Love is...

Not...

Appropriate for ages 9 to 12

Background and Border:

Cover bulletin board with white or pink felt, fabric or paper. Duplicate the Valentine border and corner from pages 62 and 63 onto white paper and color hearts with pink and red markers. Mount on edge of bulletin board. If desired, mount ruffled lace trim around edge of bulletin board so it extends beyond Valentine border.

Materials and Instructions:

Duplicate picture of Jesus from page 43 onto white paper. Color with markers, if desired. Glue or tape ruffled lace trim around the edge of the picture of Jesus. Then cut a rectangle of red construction paper approximately 11 by 13 1/2 inches and glue picture of Jesus in center of rectangle so rectangle forms a frame for the picture of Jesus and the lace trim.

Cut lettering from pages 44-45 out of red construction paper, or duplicate lettering onto pink or red paper and use in strip form. See below for making hearts.

Teaching with this Bulletin Board:

Cut one heart out of red or pink construction paper for each child. (You may wish to use the patterns on page 40.) Discuss and learn the Bible Memory Verse together. Ask each child to write on his or her heart one way he or she can show others Christ's love. Alternate method: Have each child glue his or her picture to the center of the heart and write his or her name and one way he or she will show love.

Suggested Bible Memory Verse:

"Love one another, as I have loved you." — John 15:12

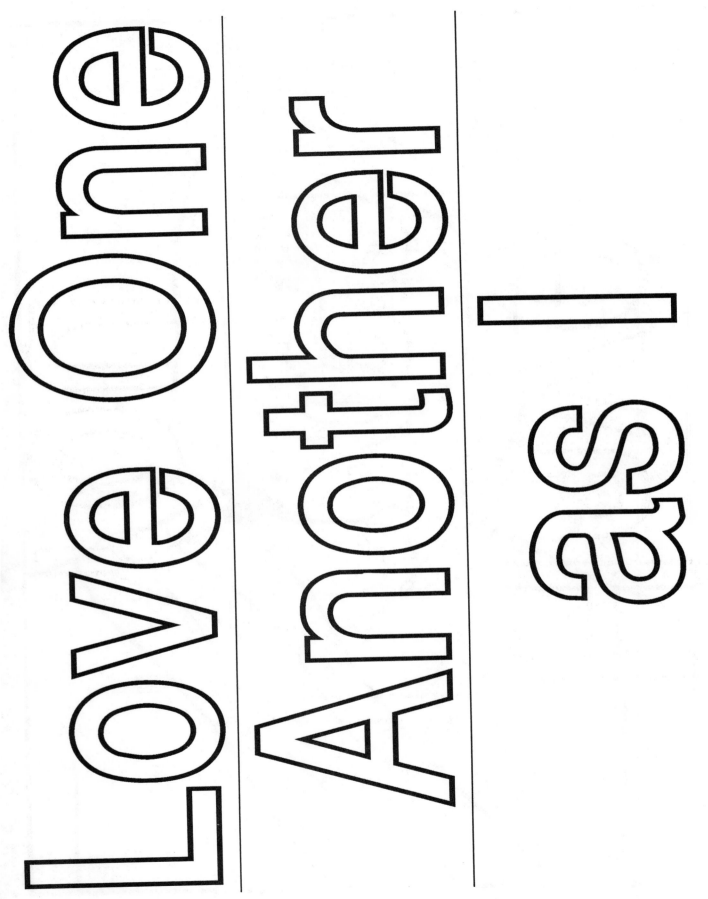

Have Loved You

Appropriate for ages 10 to 12

Background and Border:

Cover bulletin board with white fabric, felt or paper. (A fabric or wrapping paper with a tiny red or pink print on the white background looks very nice.) Duplicate the Valentine border and corner from pages 62 and 63 onto colored paper, or onto white paper and color with red and pink markers.

Materials and Instructions:

Cut a large heart out of poster board. Bend five white chenille wires into spring shapes and glue to the large heart.

Duplicate five hearts from page 47 onto pink or red paper and cut out. On each heart write one of the characteristics from Philippians 4:8: truth, honesty, justice, purity, loveliness. Tape the back of each heart to one of the chenille-wire springs. Mount the large red heart on the bulletin board.

Cut the lettering from pages 48 and 49 out of red construction paper. Or duplicate the lettering onto pink or red paper and use in strip form. If desired, short springs made from half-length chenille wires could be put behind each letter or word to give a three-dimensional effect also.

Teaching with this Bulletin Board:

Discuss each of the attributes from the Bible Memory Verse. Be sure the children understand what each means. (Explain that boys, as well as girls, can be lovely when they serve Jesus.) Relate each attribute to the children's everyday lives. Review the verse together until the children know it.

Suggested Bible Memory Verse:

"Whatsoever things are true, whatsoever things are honest, whatsoever things are just, whatsoever things are pure, whatsoever things are lovely, . . . think on these things." — Philippians 4:8

Hearts:
Duplicate five onto pink or red paper.

47

Let
These
Spring

From

Your

Heart

Appropriate for ages 8 to 12

Background and Border:

Cover bulletin board with yellow paper or fabric. (Corrugated paper or burlap would give nice texture to this bulletin board.) Use dark blue corrugated border or cut strips of dark blue construction paper into scalloped shape. Strips of dark blue crepe paper pleated and stapled around the bulletin board would also be an attractive border.

Materials and Instructions:

Duplicate smiling faces from page 51 onto colored paper, or onto white paper and color with markers. Glue on yarn scraps for hair and put ribbon bows in selected girl's hair.

If desired, cut bow ties and collars, as shown above, out of fabric or paper and glue in place. (One or two collars made of lace trim would be nice too.)

Attach faces to bulletin board in a pleasing arrangement.

Cut lettering from pages 52 and 53 out of dark blue paper or felt and staple in place. Or duplicate lettering onto colored paper and use in strip form.

Teaching with this Bulletin Board:

Discuss and learn the Bible Memory Verse together. Talk about the reasons we should be happy and smiling if we are serving God. Then discuss ways the children can share their happiness and the Gospel message with others. (If the children do not know the meaning of contagious and epidemic, be sure to explain.)

Suggested Bible Memory Verse:

"Happy is that people, whose God is the Lord." — Psalm 144:15

Smiling faces:
Duplicate onto colored paper, or onto white paper
and color with markers. Glue on yarn scraps for hair.

Smiles are

Contagious!

Start an

Epidemic

This

Winter!

Appropriate for ages 7 to 11

Background and Border:

Cover bulletin board with light blue felt or flannel. Use cotton batting to make a snow drift along bottom of board. Put crumpled newspaper behind the batting to make it stand away from the bulletin board for a three-dimensional effect. Duplicate the Wintertime border and corner from pages 62 and 63 onto colored paper or onto white paper and color with markers.

Materials and Instructions:

Duplicate the snowman's head from page 57 onto white paper or poster board and cut out. If desired, glue cotton batting to snowman's head. Glue on black pompoms for eyes and nose. Color in smile with red marker.

Cut large circle about 16 inches in diameter out of white paper or poster board for the snowman's body. Outline with black marker. Glue actual twigs behind the body to form arms. If desired, glue cotton batting to snowman's body. Staple head and body to bulletin board.

Trace the snowman's hat from page 56 onto black paper or felt and cut out. Glue on a piece of red ribbon or a strip of paper or felt as a hat band. Staple hat to bulletin board.

Use a piece of plaid or striped fabric, or an actual child's scarf, as the snowman's scarf. Pin in place on the bulletin board.

Cut lettering from page 55 out of dark blue felt or paper and staple in place. Or duplicate the lettering onto blue paper and use in strip form.

Teaching with this Bulletin Board:

Talk about the joy God gives us. Emphasize that we can only know real joy after we have accepted Jesus as our Savior. Present the plan of salvation and give the opportunity for children to accept Jesus. Learn the Bible Memory Verse together.

Suggested Bible Memory Verse:

"The joy of the Lord is your strength." —Nehemiah 8:10

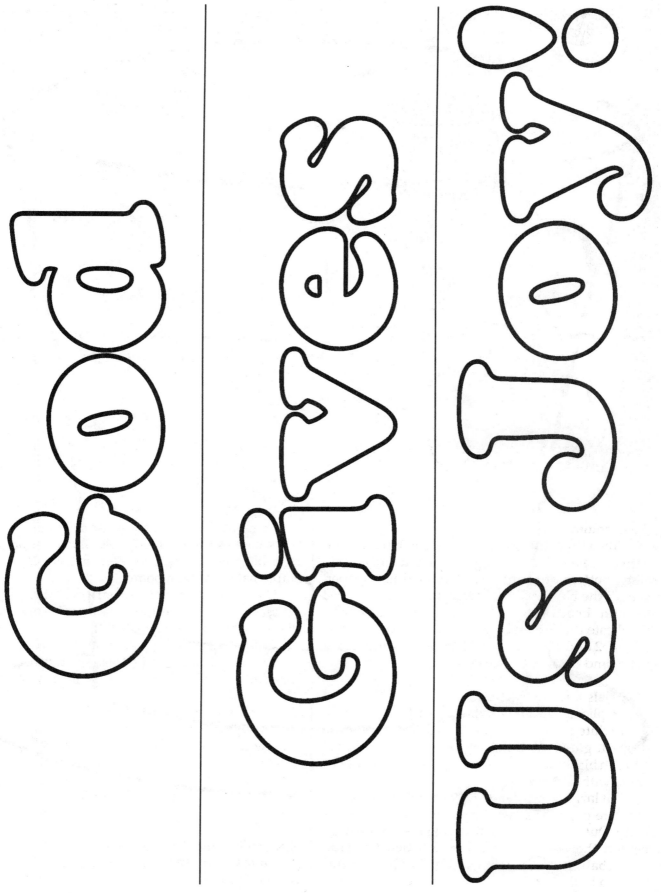

Snowman's hat:
Trace onto black paper or felt and cut out. Cut piece of
red ribbon or strip of paper or felt for hat band.

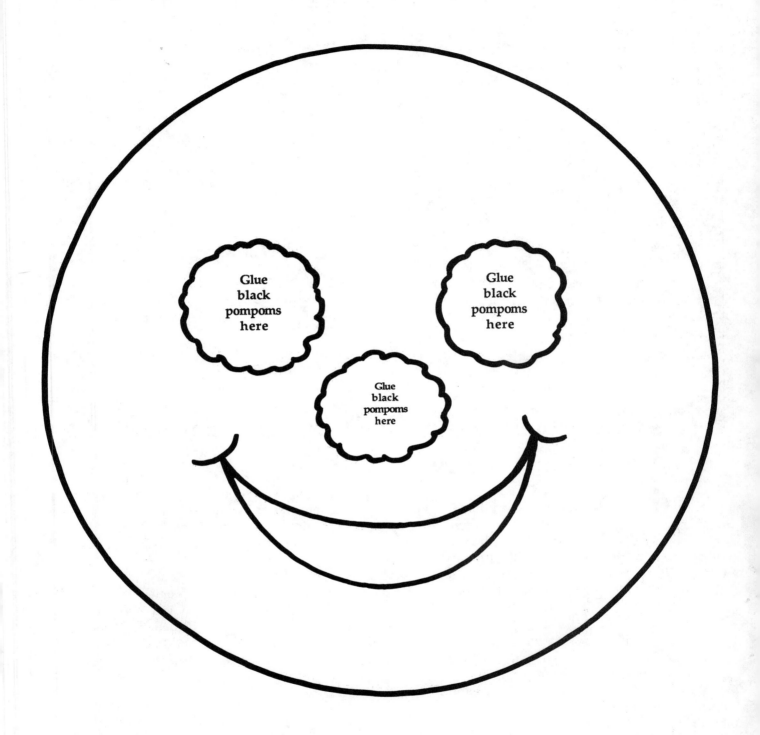

Snowman's head:
Duplicate onto white paper and cut out. Color in smile with red marker. Glue on black pompoms for eyes and nose.

Appropriate for ages 4 to 10

Background and Border:

Cover bulletin board with dark blue felt, paper or fabric. Duplicate Wintertime border and corner from pages 62 and 63 and color with markers, or duplicate onto colored paper. An alternative border could be made by taping rounded strips of cotton batting along bulletin board frame.

Materials and Instructions:

Cut a variety of sizes, shapes and designs of snowflakes from white tissue paper or paper napkins using the instructions on page 59.

Lay snowflakes flat on newspaper and lightly spray with artist's adhesive and sprinkle with glitter (or use spray-on glitter).

Mount snowflakes on bulletin board with tiny spots of glue in each point of the snowflakes.

Cut lettering from pages 60 and 61 out of white paper. If desired, glue on cotton balls or cotton batting. Cover with glitter. Attach to bulletin board.

Teaching with this Bulletin Board:

Learn the Bible Memory Verse together. Talk about the different seasons God made. Discuss why God created snow and its benefits to us. Have the children name other "good and perfect gifts" God gives us during the various seasons.

Suggested Bible Memory Verse:

"Every good gift and every perfect gift is from above, and cometh down from the Father." — James 1:17

Instructions for cutting snowflakes:
Use squares of white tissue paper or paper napkins.

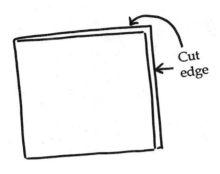

1. Fold square into quarters.

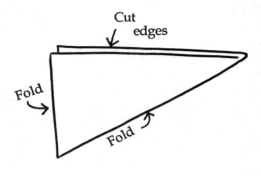

2. Fold in half diagonally to form triangle.

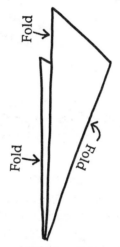

3. Fold triangle in half again to form thin triangle.

4. Cut off wide end of triangle in point.

5. Cut out triangles, half circles and other designs along pointed outside edge and folded edges, being careful to not cut folded edge completely. Cut off tip of triangle.

6. Unfold snowflake.

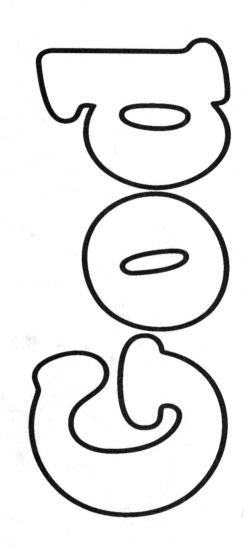

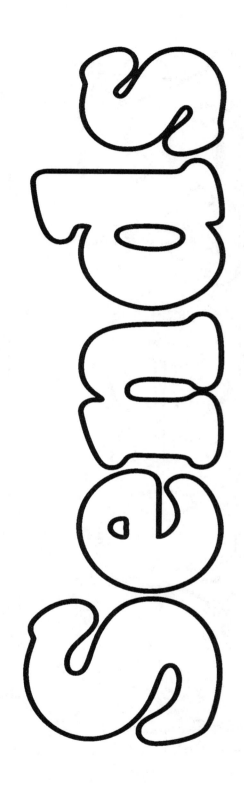

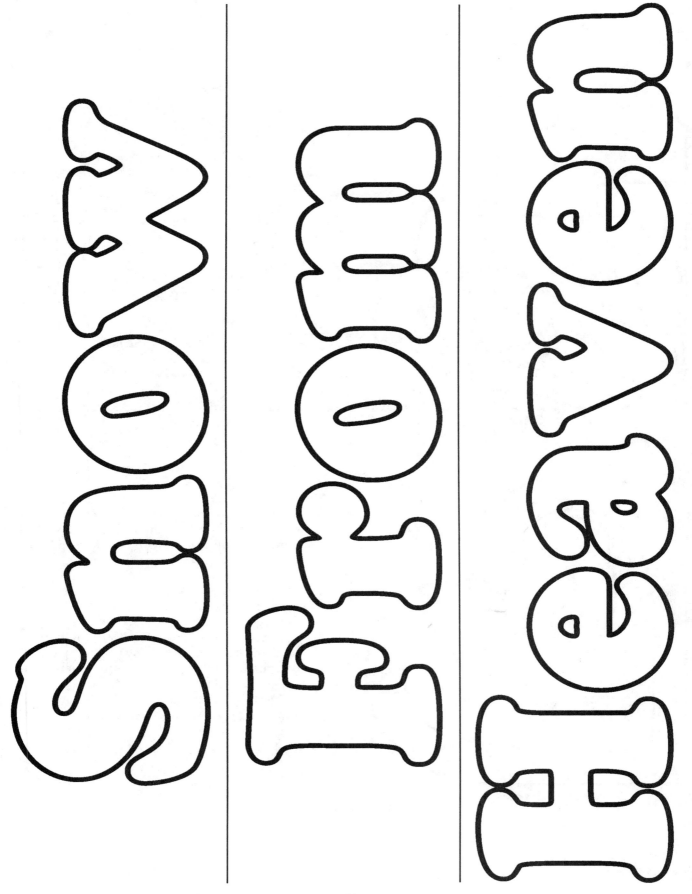

Christmas Corner

Wintertime Corner

Valentine Corner

How to Use Winter
Borders and Corners

Choose the border you wish to use. Duplicate enough copies of that border strip to cover the entire frame of your bulletin board. In addition, make four copies of the matching corner.

You may duplicate the borders and corners onto white paper and color in the borders with markers. (The children will enjoy helping you do this.)

Or you may wish to duplicate the borders and corners onto colored copy machine paper or construction paper which compliments the background colors in the bulletin board.

Overlap the border strips slightly and glue or tape the sections together. Roll the border to store for future use.

Christmas Border   Wintertime Border   Valentine Border

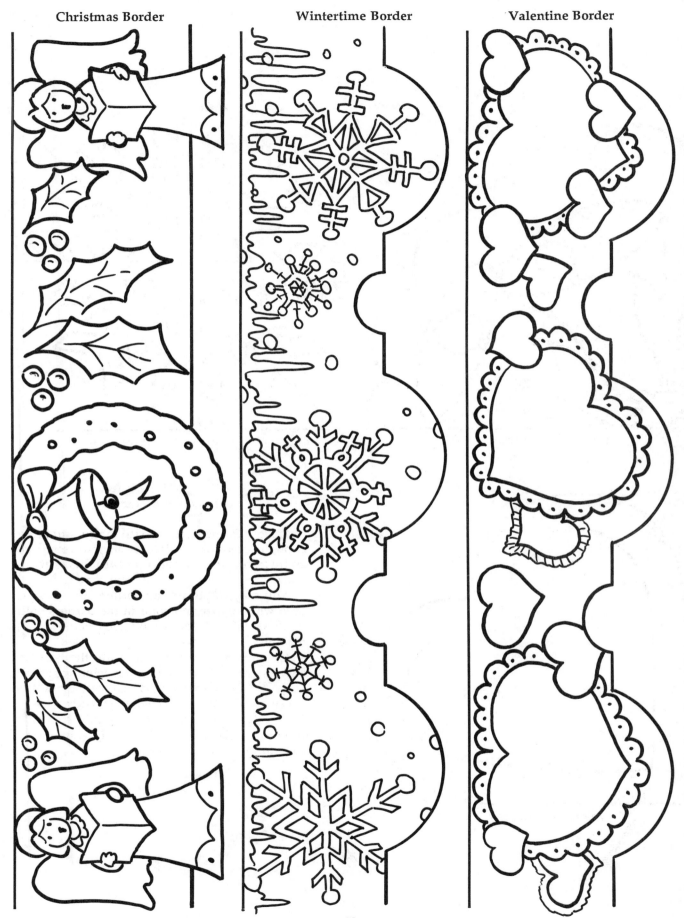